learn to creat
Felt Pincushions

Topped with quilt-inspired designs, these colorful pincushions are beautiful and useful gifts. The 4" square or round shapes are the perfect size to keep in handy spots throughout the home. Quality felt makes them long-lasting and easy to create.

10 12 14

16 18 20 22

24 26 28 30

LEISURE ARTS, INC. • Maumelle, Arkansas

Pincushion Basics

To make assembling your pincushion easier and more enjoyable, we encourage you to carefully read all of the **Pincushion Basics**, study the color photographs, and familiarize yourself with the individual project instructions before beginning.

GENERAL SUPPLIES

FELT
There are several types of felt available. The most common types are 100% wool, wool/rayon blend, and 100% polyester craft felt. Any of these are suitable for your pincushion. If you want your pincushion to last for years, use 100% wool or wool/rayon blend felt. These are sturdy and wear-resistant.

Do not wash the felt before use. Doing so will change the felted quality and colors may bleed when the felt comes in contact with water. If your felt has a wrinkle, press lightly with a warm dry iron.

The cut edges of felt do not ravel so seams can be left unfinished on the outside of the pincushion.

FILLING
For a lightweight, fast-to-make pincushion, simply place about $1/2$ cup of polypropylene pellets directly in the pincushion and fill the remainder of the pincushion with polyester fiberfill. Polypropylene pellets and fiberfill are available at sewing and craft stores.

If you desire a weighted pincushion that will stay in place when you're using it and will be long-lasting, you will want to make an inner pincushion and fill it with emery sand or crushed walnut shells.

Emery sand is an excellent product for filling your pincushion and it helps keep pins and needles sharp. You can find it at larger hardware stores where it's sold with supplies for sand blasting. There are also sources online that sell small quantities just for filling pincushions.

Crushed walnut shells are another good product to use for filling your pincushion. They are sold at pet stores for bedding. This material is a bit more coarse than emery sand yet adds a nice weighted feel. This **would not** be a good choice for someone who is allergic to nuts.

THREAD, FLOSS, OR PEARL COTTON

If you are making an inner pincushion, you will need a sewing machine and all-purpose sewing thread. Match the thread color to the fabric color.

To construct the pincushion by machine, you will need all-purpose sewing thread. Be sure to use the same color in the bobbin and the needle. Match the thread color to the felt color or choose a contrasting color.

To construct the pincushion by hand, use three strands of embroidery floss or 1 strand of #5, #8, or #12 pearl cotton. Embroidery floss comes with 6 strands twisted together in a skein. Prepare the embroidery floss by separating all the strands and aligning the required number of strands before use. Do not try to separate the pearl cotton; use it as it comes off the skein or ball. Match the floss or pearl cotton color to the fabric or felt color or choose a contrasting color.

PLASTIC COATED FREEZER PAPER

Use freezer paper for cutting out the felt pieces. It has a paper side, perfect for tracing your patterns onto, and a plastic side that can be temporarily adhered to your felt with an iron.

GLUE

Use a fabric glue stick or a small drop of fabric glue to tack the appliqués to the top before sewing in place.

SCISSORS OR ROTARY CUTTER, CUTTING MAT, AND QUILTING RULER

When using felt, very sharp cutting equipment is a must for precisely cutting your pieces. Sharp scissors or a rotary cutter are excellent choices. Most of the pieces can be quickly and accurately cut with rotary cutting equipment but scissors are easier to use when cutting curved pieces.

FABRIC FOR INNER PINCUSHION (OPTIONAL)

If using emery sand or crushed walnut shells to fill your pincushion, an inner pincushion will prevent the fine emery sand or crushed walnut shells from working out of the pincushion with use. Choose a tightly woven fabric, such as drapery lining, to make the inner pincushion.

SEWING MACHINE (OPTIONAL)

A sewing machine is needed for making an inner pincushion and can be used for making the pincushion. Begin with a new needle (size 70 or 80). Set the machine stitch length to either 2.5 or 3 (11 or 9 stitches per inch, respectively). Clean the bobbin casing regularly as you sew to remove the lint that might accumulate there.

CHENILLE NEEDLES (OPTIONAL)

The size chenille needle you need depends on the size pearl cotton or number of embroidery floss strands you are using.
- Size 24 for 1-2 strands of embroidery floss
- Size 22 for #12 pearl cotton or 3-4 strands of embroidery floss
- Size 20 for #8 pearl cotton or 5-6 strands of embroidery floss
- Size 18 for #5 pearl cotton

EMBROIDERY SCISSORS (OPTIONAL)

A very small pair of sharp scissors made just for embroidery will make clipping your thread ends easy and accurate.

CUTTING

Follow the project instructions to cut all the pieces for the pincushion from felt and, if desired, for the inner pincushion from fabric.

Use a black permanent pen to trace each pattern piece onto the paper side of freezer paper the number of times indicated in the project instructions. Leave a bit of space between each piece. Cut each piece slightly outside the drawn line and iron the plastic side of the freezer paper to the felt. Cut the pieces out along the drawn lines. Sharp scissors or rotary cutting equipment can be used to cut pieces quickly, easily, and precisely. Remove the freezer paper.

Tip: When the pincushion top is a dark color and there are small, lighter color pieces stitched to it (for example, Pole Star, page 22), sometimes the darker color of the top will show through the gaps between the pieces. To avoid this, put a lighter color of felt between the pincushion top and the pieces. Trace the outline of the complete shape formed by the pieces (for example, the octagon) and cut the shape slightly smaller from the lighter color felt.

ADDING THE APPLIQUÉS TO THE PINCUSHION TOP

1. To find the center, fold the felt top (**A**) in half; fold in half again. Place a pin through the felt at the center point; unfold the top.
2. Referring to the pattern, center and arrange the appliqué pieces on the top. When you are pleased with the arrangement, lift each piece and apply a small dab of glue to the underside. Use the smallest amount of glue you can so the dried glue does not interfere with sewing the appliqués to the top.
3. Sew each appliqué piece in place by using a sewing machine and sewing thread *or* by hand with a Running Stitch using three strands of embroidery floss *or* one strand of #5, #8, or #12 pearl cotton. Work the stitches about $1/16$" away from the edge. Pull all thread ends to the back of the top and knot.

ASSEMBLING AN INNER PINCUSHION

FLAT INNER PINCUSHION
*Match **right** sides and raw edges and use a sewing machine with all-purpose sewing thread and a $1/4$" seam allowance to make the inner pincushion.*

1. Sew the inner pincushion top and the inner pincushion bottom together, leaving about a 1" opening.
2. Turn the inner pincushion right side out. Fill with emery sand or crushed walnut shells. Sew the opening closed.

DIMENSIONAL INNER PINCUSHION

Square Inner Pincushion
*Match **right** sides and raw edges and use a sewing machine with all-purpose sewing thread and a $1/4$" seam allowance to make the inner pincushion.*

1. Press one short end of the inner pincushion sides $1/4$" to the wrong side. Begin with the pressed end in the center of one edge of the inner pincushion top and sew the top to the inner pincushion sides along one edge. When you reach the first corner, stop $1/4$" from the corner; pivot. Reposition the sides under the next edge and continue sewing. Sew the top to the sides, pivoting at each corner and repositioning the sides under the next edge of the top. Trimming as needed, overlap the ends about $1/4$". Whipstitch the ends together.

2. Fold the inner pincushion bottom in half; mark the folds with pins. Match the pins and fold in half again; mark with pins. Do the same for the inner pincushion sides by locating where the corners are, folding and placing pins at the center of each side. Match the pins on the bottom to the pins on the side edges; pin *(Fig. 1)*.

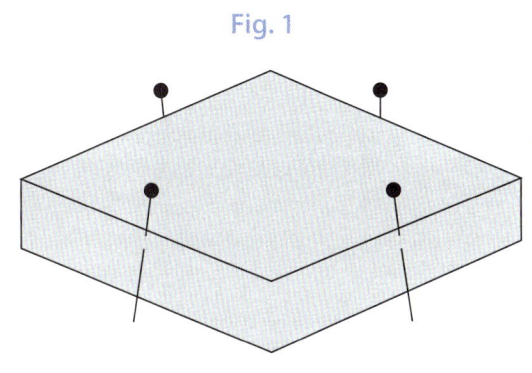

Fig. 1

3. Sew the bottom and sides together, leaving about a 1" opening. Turn the inner pincushion right side out. Fill with emery sand or crushed walnut shells. Sew the opening closed.

Round Inner Pincushion
*Match **right** sides and raw edges and use a sewing machine with all-purpose sewing thread and a 1/4" seam allowance to make the inner pincushion.*

1. Press one short end of the inner pincushion sides 1/4" to the wrong side. Begin with the pressed end where desired on the edge of the inner pincushion top and sew the top to the inner pincushion sides. Trimming as needed, overlap the side ends about 1/4". Whipstitch the ends together.
2. Fold the inner pincushion bottom in half; mark the folds with pins. Match the pins and fold in half again; mark with pins. Do the same for the inner pincushion sides, folding and placing pins to divide the sides into four equal sections. Match the pins on the bottom to the pins on the side edges; pin *(Fig. 2)*.

Fig. 2

3. Sew the bottom and sides together, leaving about a 1" opening. Turn the inner pincushion right side out. Fill with emery sand or crushed walnut shells. Sew the opening closed.

ASSEMBLING THE PINCUSHION

FLAT PINCUSHION
*A flat pincushion can be assembled by machine and then embellished with Blanket Stitches **or** by pinking the edges. It can also be assembled by hand with Blanket Stitches only.*

By Machine
Use all-purpose sewing thread and a 1/4" seam allowance to make the pincushion.

1. Place the felt pincushion top and pincushion bottom (**A**), **wrong** sides together.
2. Sew around the edges, leaving about 1" open on one edge if filling with polypropylene pellets and fiberfill *or* an entire edge open for inserting a flat inner pincushion.
3. Fill with polypropylene pellets and fiberfill *or* insert a flat inner pincushion; sew the opening closed.
4. If desired, work Blanket Stitches about 1/4" wide and 1/4" deep on the outer edges with one 36" strand of #5, #8, or #12 pearl cotton or three 36" strands of embroidery floss (see **Tip**, page 6) *or* use pinking shears to trim the edges.

By Hand

Use one 36" strand of #5, #8, or #12 pearl cotton or three 36" strands of embroidery floss to make the pincushion. Always work with the pincushion top up so you can easily see your stitches to space them evenly.

1. Place the felt pincushion top and pincushion bottom (**A**) **wrong** sides together.
2. Work Blanket Stitches about 1/4" wide and 1/4" deep around the edges, leaving about 1" open on one edge if filling with polypropylene pellets and fiberfill *or* an entire edge open for inserting a flat inner pincushion. Do not cut the pearl cotton or embroidery floss.
3. Fill with polypropylene pellets and fiberfill *or* insert a flat inner pincushion; Blanket Stitch the opening closed.

SQUARE DIMENSIONAL PINCUSHION

A square dimensional pincushion can be assembled by machine and then embellished with Blanket Stitches. It can also be assembled by hand with Blanket Stitches only.

By Machine

*Match **wrong** sides and raw edges and use a sewing machine with all-purpose sewing thread and a 1/4" seam allowance to make the pincushion.*

1. If piecing the pincushion sides, overlap one short end of each side piece 1/4" and Whipstitch the pieces together with embroidery floss or pearl cotton as indicated in the project instructions.
2. Beginning with one end of the sides in the center of one edge of the top (**A**), sew the top to the pincushion sides along one edge. When you reach the first corner, stop 1/4" from the corner; pivot. Reposition the sides under the next edge and continue sewing. Sew the top to the sides, pivoting at each corner and repositioning the sides under the next edge of the top. Trimming as needed, overlap the side ends about 1/4". Whipstitch the ends together.
3. Fold the bottom (**A**) in half; mark the folds with pins. Match the pins and fold in half again; mark with pins. Do the same for the pincushion sides by locating where the corners are, folding and placing pins at the center of each side. Match the pins on the bottom to the pins on the side edges; pin *(Fig. 4)*.

Fig. 4

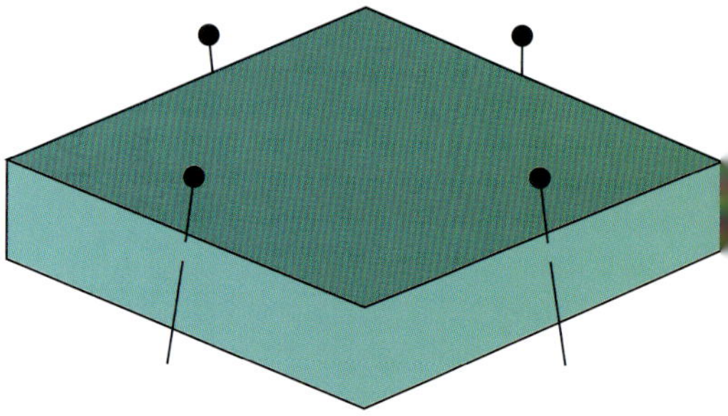

4. Repeat Step 2 to sew the bottom and sides together, leaving about a 1" opening if filling with polypropylene pellets and fiberfill *or* an entire edge open for inserting a square inner pincushion.
5. Fill with polypropylene pellets and fiberfill *or* insert a square inner pincushion; sew the opening closed.
6. Work Blanket Stitches about 1/4" wide and 1/4" deep on the edges with one 36" strand of #5, #8, or #12 pearl cotton *or* three 36" strands of embroidery floss (see **Tip**).

Tip: Use the machine-stitched seam as a guide, placing the Blanket Stitches every second or third machine stitch *(Fig. 3)*.

Fig 3

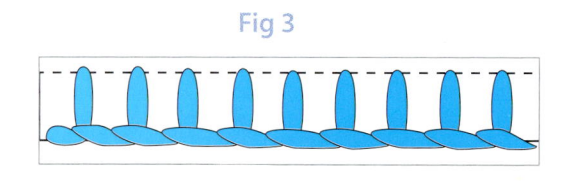

By Hand
*Match **wrong** sides and raw edges and use one 36" strand of #5, #8, or #12 pearl cotton or three 36" strands of embroidery floss to make the pincushion. Always work with the pincushion top up so you can easily see your stitches to space them evenly.*

1. If piecing the pincushion sides, overlap one short end of each side piece 1/4" and Whipstitch the pieces together with embroidery floss or pearl cotton as indicated in the project instructions.
2. Beginning with one end of the sides in the center of one edge of the top (**A**), pin one long edge to the pincushion sides. Work Blanket Stitches about 1/4" wide and 1/4" deep on the outer edges. When you reach the first corner, take a diagonal stitch at the corner. Reposition the sides under the next edge and continue stitching all the way around the top, taking a diagonal stitch at each corner and repositioning the sides under the next edge of the top. Trimming as needed, overlap the ends by about 1/4". Whipstitch the ends together.
3. Fold the bottom (**A**) in half; mark the folds with pins. Match the pins and fold in half again; mark with pins. Do the same for the pincushion sides by locating where the corners are, folding and placing pins at the center of each side. Match the pins on the bottom to the pins on the side edges; pin (see **Fig. 4**).
4. Blanket Stitch the bottom and sides together, leaving about a 1" opening if filling with polypropylene pellets and fiberfill *or* an entire edge open for inserting a square inner pincushion. Do not cut the pearl cotton or embroidery floss.
5. Fill with polypropylene pellets and fiberfill *or* insert a square inner pincushion; Blanket Stitch the opening closed.

ROUND DIMENSIONAL PINCUSHION
A round dimensional pincushion can be assembled by machine and then embellished with Blanket Stitches. It can also be assembled by hand with Blanket Stitches only.

By Machine
*Match **wrong** sides and raw edges and use a sewing machine with all-purpose sewing thread and a 1/4" seam allowance to make the pincushion.*

1. If piecing the pincushion sides, overlap one short end of each side piece 1/4" and Whipstitch the pieces together with embroidery floss or pearl cotton as indicated in the project instructions.
2. Beginning where desired, sew the edge of the top (**A**) to the pincushion sides along one edge. Trimming as needed, overlap the ends about 1/4". Whipstitch the ends together.
3. Fold the bottom (**A**) in half; mark the folds with pins. Match the pins and fold in half again; mark with pins. Do the same for the pincushion sides, folding and placing pins to divide the sides into four equal sections. Match the pins on the bottom to the pins on the side edges; pin (**Fig. 5**).
4. Sew the bottom and sides together, leaving about a 1" opening if filling with polypropylene pellets and fiberfill *or* about half of the side edge open for inserting a round inner pincushion.
5. Fill with polypropylene pellets and fiberfill *or* insert a round inner pincushion; sew the opening closed.
6. Work Blanket Stitches about 1/4" wide and 1/4" deep on the edges with one 36" strand of #5, #8, or #12 pearl cotton *or* three 36" strands of embroidery floss (see **Tip**, page 6).

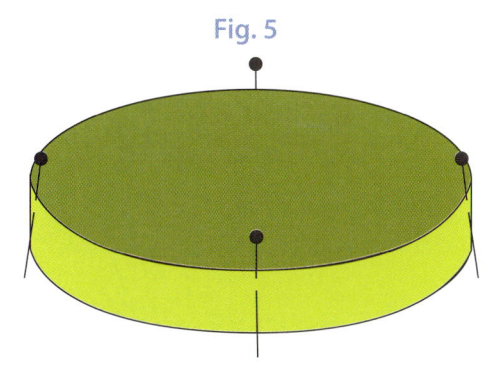

By Hand
*Match **wrong** sides and raw edges and use one 36" strand of #5, #8, or #12 pearl cotton or three 36" strands of embroidery floss to make the pincushion. Always work with the pincushion top up so you can easily see your stitches to space them evenly.*

1. If piecing the pincushion sides, overlap one short end of each side piece 1/4" and Whipstitch the pieces together with embroidery floss or pearl cotton as indicated in the project instructions.
2. Beginning where desired, pin the edge of the top (**A**) to the pincushion sides along one edge. Work Blanket Stitches about 1/4" wide and 1/4" deep on the outer edges. Trimming as needed, overlap the ends by about 1/4". Whipstitch the ends together.

Fig. 5

3. Fold the bottom (**A**) in half; mark the folds with pins. Match the pins and fold in half again; mark with pins. Do the same for the pincushion sides, folding and placing pins to divide the sides into four equal sections. Match the pins on the bottom to the pins on the side edges; pin (see **Fig. 5**).
4. Blanket Stitch the bottom and sides together, leaving about a 1" opening if filling with polypropylene pellets and fiberfill *or* about half of the side edge open for inserting a round inner pincushion. Do not cut the pearl cotton or embroidery floss.
5. Fill with polypropylene pellets and fiberfill *or* insert a round inner pincushion; Blanket Stitch the opening closed.

HAND STITCHES

BLANKET STITCH

Bring the pearl cotton or embroidery floss up between two pieces, catching a small bit of felt inside to anchor the knot. Working to the right, place the needle as shown, stitching into the felt. Keeping the pearl cotton or embroidery floss below the point of the needle and stitching through both layers of felt, go down at 2 and come up at 3 *(Fig. 6)* and tug gently to close the stitch. Continue working in the same manner, going down at even numbers and coming up at odd numbers *(Fig. 7)*.

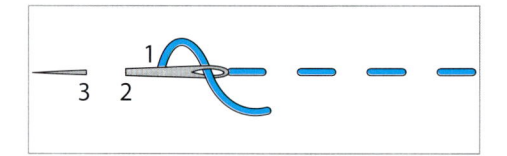

Fig. 6

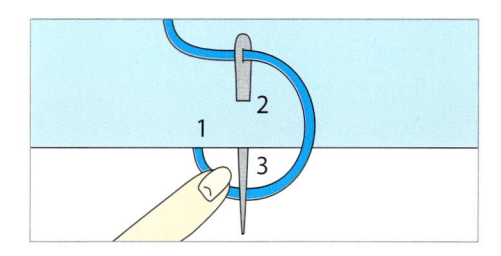

Fig. 7

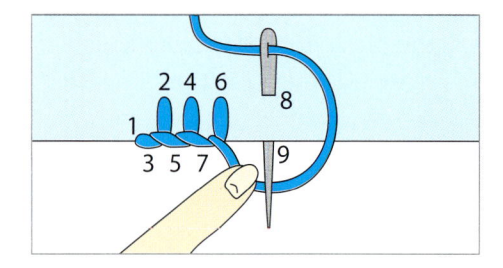

RUNNING STITCH

"Stab" the needle straight up and down through the felt to work the neatest stitches. Come up at 1, go down at 2, and come up at 3 *(Fig. 8)*. Continue working in the same manner, trying to make the stitches the same length and the same distance apart.

Fig. 8

FRENCH KNOT

Bring needle up at 1. Wrap pearl cotton or embroidery floss around needle. Insert needle at 2, tighten knot, and pull needle through felt, holding pearl cotton or embroidery floss until it must be released *(Fig. 9)*.

Fig. 9

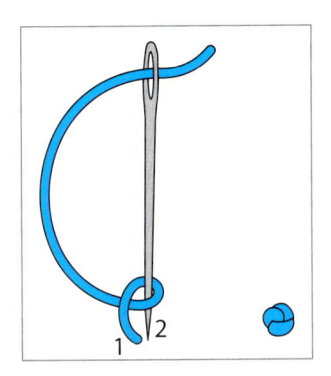

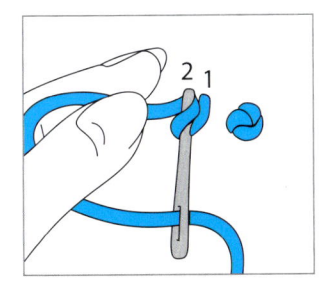

STRAIGHT STITCH

"Stab" the needle straight up and down through the felt to work the neatest stitches. Come up at 1, go down at 2 *(Fig.10)*.

Fig. 10

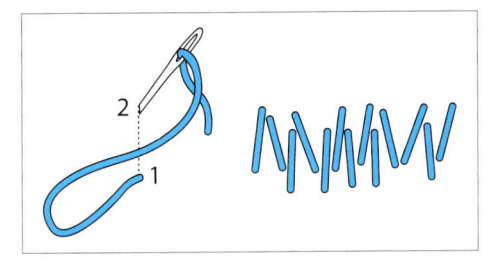

WHIPSTITCH

Come up at 1. Go down at 2, directly across from 1 *(Fig. 11)*. Come up at 3, approximately $1/16$" below 1. Continue working in the same manner, coming up at odd numbers and going down at even numbers.

Fig. 11

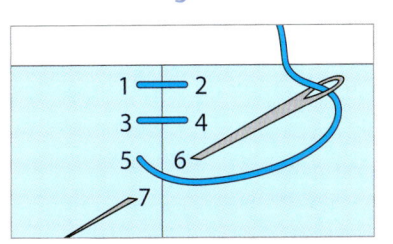

9

Friendship Star

Shopping List

- ☐ 4" x 4" piece of light pink felt for bottom (**A**)
- ☐ 4" x 4" piece of pink felt for top (**A**)
- ☐ 1 1/8" x 1 1/8" piece of yellow felt for star center (**B**)
- ☐ 2" x 3" piece of green felt for star points
- ☐ 6" x 10" piece of fabric for inner pincushion (optional)
- ☐ sewing thread to match pink, yellow, and green felt
- ☐ pinking shears (optional)
- ☐ general supplies

CUTTING

Measurements include 1/4" seam allowances where needed. Pieces can be cut as listed or using the pattern, below.

From green felt:
- Cut 2 squares 1 1/8" x 1 1/8". Cut each square diagonally to make a total of 4 **triangles** (**C**).

From fabric for inner pincushion:
- Cut **top** 4" x 4".
- Cut **bottom** 4" x 4".

ASSEMBLY

1. Add appliqués to the **top** (**A**). We stitched the appliqués in place with the sewing machine using thread to match the appliqués.
2. Unless filling with polypropylene pellets and fiberfill, make a flat inner pincushion.
3. Make and fill a flat pincushion. We used the sewing machine with sewing thread to match the top and pinking shears to trim the edges.

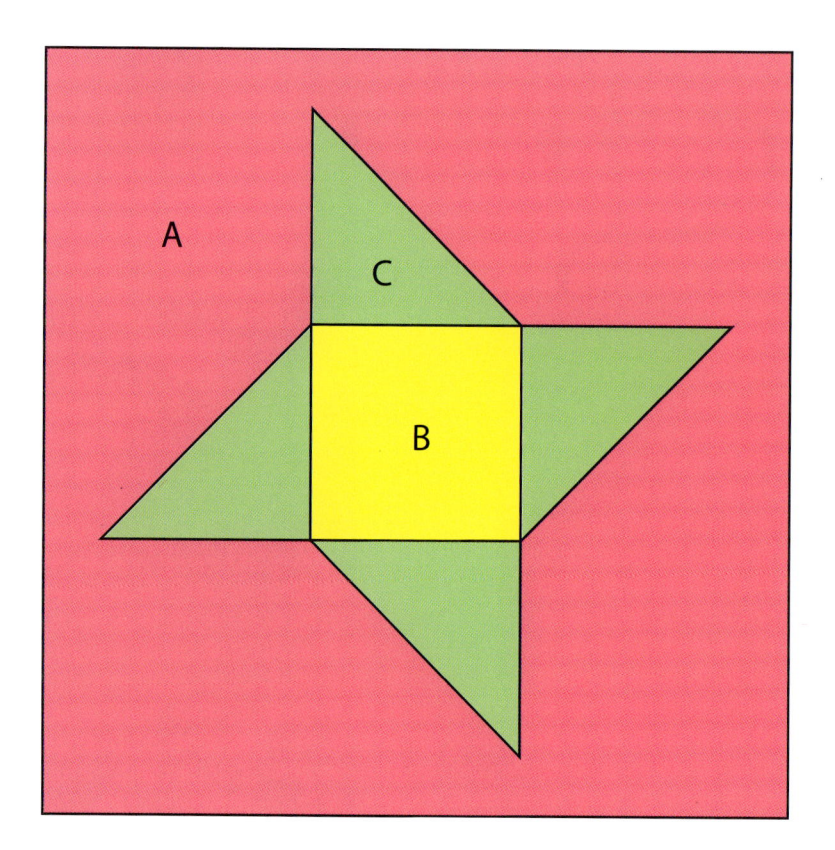

11

Flying Geese

Shopping List

- ☐ 4" x 4" piece of medium blue felt for top (A)
- ☐ 5" x 6" piece of light green felt for bottom and triangles
- ☐ 2" x 3" piece of medium green felt for triangles
- ☐ 6" x 10" piece of fabric for inner pincushion (optional)
- ☐ embroidery floss to match light green and medium green felt
- ☐ #5 pearl cotton to match medium green felt
- ☐ general supplies

CUTTING

Measurements include 1/4" seam allowances where needed. Pieces can be cut as listed or using the pattern, below.

From light green felt:
- Cut **bottom** 4" x 4" (**A**).
- Cut 2 squares $1\frac{1}{8}$" x $1\frac{1}{8}$". Cut each square diagonally to make a total of 4 **triangles** (**B**).

From medium green felt:
- Cut 2 squares $1\frac{1}{8}$" x $1\frac{1}{8}$". Cut each square diagonally to make a total of 4 **triangles** (**B**).

From fabric for inner pincushion:
- Cut **top** 4" x 4".
- Cut **bottom** 4" x 4".

ASSEMBLY

1. Add appliqués to the **top** (**A**). We used a Running Stitch with 2 strands of embroidery floss to match the appliqués.
2. Unless filling with polypropylene pellets and fiberfill, make a flat inner pincushion.
3. Make and fill a flat pincushion. We used the sewing machine with sewing thread to match the top and added Blanket Stitches around the outer edges with pearl cotton.

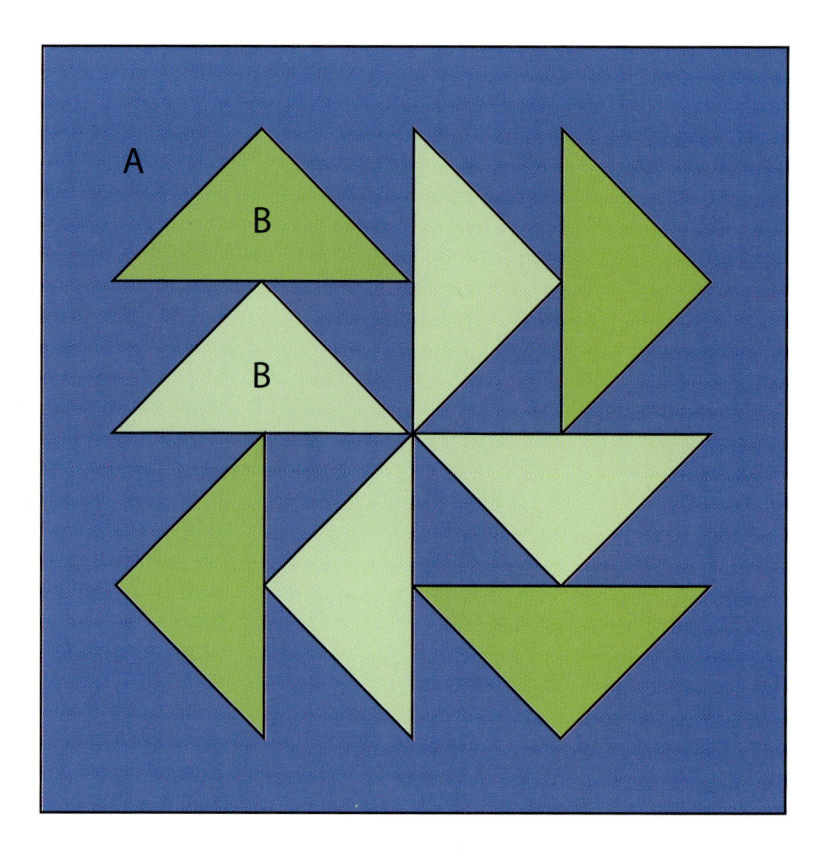

13

Four Leaf Clover

Shopping List

- ☐ 4" x 4" piece of white felt for top (A)
- ☐ 4" x 17" *or* 5" x 10" piece of green felt for sides and clovers
- ☐ 4" x 4" piece of blue felt for bottom (A)
- ☐ 6" x 18" piece of fabric for inner pincushion (optional)
- ☐ embroidery floss to match green felt
- ☐ general supplies

CUTTING

Measurements include 1/4" seam allowances where needed. Pieces can be cut as listed or using the pattern, below.

From green felt:
- Cut **sides** 1 1/4" x 17" *or* 2 sides 1 1/4" x 9".
- Use pattern to cut 4 **clovers** (**B**).

From fabric for inner pincushion:
- Cut **sides** 1 1/4" x 17".
- Cut **top** 4" x 4".
- Cut **bottom** 4" x 4".

ASSEMBLY

1. Add appliqués to the **top** (**A**). We used a Running Stitch with 3 strands of embroidery floss.
2. Unless filling with polypropylene pellets and fiberfill, make a square dimensional inner pincushion.
3. Make and fill a square dimensional pincushion. We assembled the pincushion using a Blanket Stitch with 3 strands of embroidery floss.

15

Diamond Star

Shopping List

- ☐ 3" x 5" piece of bright blue felt for diamonds
- ☐ 4" x 4" piece of dark blue felt for top (A)
- ☐ 6" x 8" piece of bright green felt for bottom and triangles
- ☐ 2" x 2" piece of yellow felt for squares
- ☐ 2" x 18" *or* 3" x 9" piece of teal felt for sides
- ☐ 6" x 18" piece of fabric for inner pincushion (optional)
- ☐ embroidery floss to match bright blue, bright green, and yellow felt
- ☐ #5 pearl cotton to match bright green felt
- ☐ general supplies

CUTTING

Measurements include ¼" seam allowances where needed. Pieces can be cut as listed or using the pattern, below.

From bright blue felt:
- Use pattern to cut 4 **diamonds** (D).

From bright green felt:
- Cut **bottom** 4" x 4" (A).
- Use pattern to cut 16 **triangles** (B).

From yellow felt:
- Cut 4 **squares** ⅝" x ⅝" (C).

From teal felt:
- Cut **sides** 1¼" x 17" *or* 2 **sides** 1¼" x 9".

From fabric for inner pincushion:
- Cut **sides** 1¼" x 17".
- Cut **top** 4" x 4".
- Cut **bottom** 4" x 4".

ASSEMBLY

1. Add appliqués to the **top** (A). We used a Running Stitch with 2 strands of embroidery floss to match the appliqués.
2. Unless filling with polypropylene pellets and fiberfill, make a square dimensional inner pincushion.
3. Make and fill a square dimensional pincushion. We assembled the pincushion using a Blanket Stitch with #5 pearl cotton.

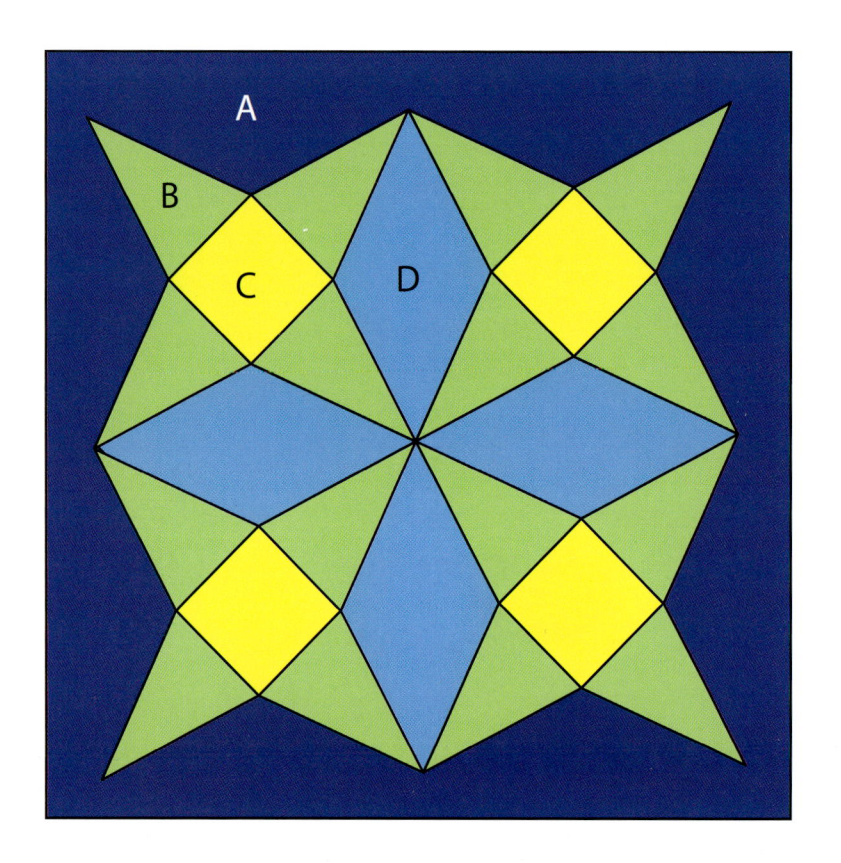

17

Geometric Stars

Shopping List

- 4" x 4" piece of white felt for top (**A**)
- 6" x 8" piece of red felt for bottom and triangles
- 4" x 18" *or* 5" x 10" piece of orange felt for sides and diamonds
- 6" x 18" piece of fabric for inner pincushion (optional)
- #8 pearl cotton to match red and orange felt
- #5 pearl cotton to match orange and white felt
- general supplies

CUTTING

Measurements include 1/4" seam allowances where needed. Pieces can be cut as listed or using the pattern, below.

From red felt:
- Cut **bottom** (**A**) 4" x 4".
- Use pattern to cut 16 **triangles** (**B**).

From orange felt:
- Cut **sides** 1 1/4" x 17" *or* 2 **sides** 1 1/4" x 9".
- Use pattern to cut 16 **diamonds** (**C**).

From fabric for inner pincushion:
- Cut **sides** 1 1/4" x 17".
- Cut **top** 4" x 4".
- Cut **bottom** 4" x 4".

ASSEMBLY

1. Add appliqués to the **top** (**A**). We used a Running Stitch with #8 pearl cotton to match the appliqués.
2. Unless filling with polypropylene pellets and fiberfill, make a square dimensional inner pincushion.
3. Make and fill a square dimensional pincushion. We assembled the pincushion using a Blanket Stitch with white #5 pearl cotton on the top and orange #5 pearl cotton on the bottom.

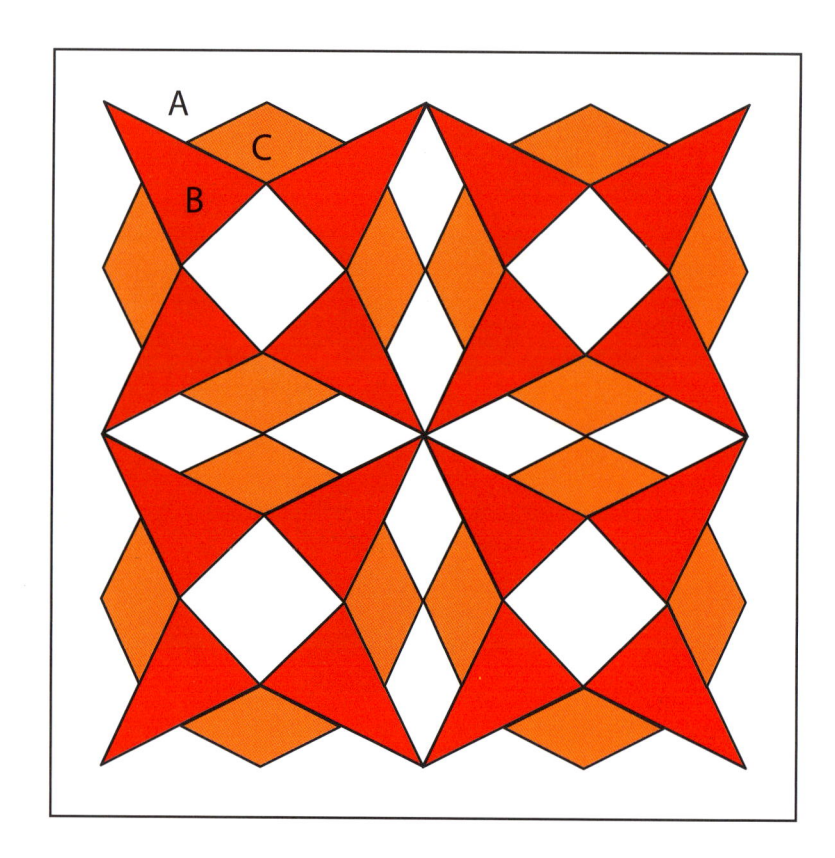

19

Purple Lily

Shopping List

- ☐ 4" x 4" piece of cream felt for top (A)
- ☐ 5" x 9" piece of light purple felt for bottom and petals
- ☐ 3" x 3" piece of dark purple felt for petals
- ☐ 3" x 18" *or* 4" x 10" piece of medium green felt for sides and stem
- ☐ 2" x 4" piece of dark green felt for leaves
- ☐ 6" x 18" piece of fabric for inner pincushion (optional)
- ☐ embroidery floss to coordinate with dark green and dark purple felt
- ☐ #5 pearl cotton to coordinate with dark purple felt
- ☐ general supplies

CUTTING

Measurements include ¼" seam allowances where needed. Pieces can be cut as listed or using the pattern, below.

From light purple felt:
- Cut **bottom (A)** 4" x 4".
- Use pattern to cut 4 **petals (B)**.

From dark purple felt:
- Use pattern to cut 4 **petals (B)**.

From medium green felt:
- Cut **sides** 1¼" x 17" *or* 2 sides 1¼" x 9".
- Use pattern to cut **stem (E)**.

From dark green felt:
- Use pattern to cut 1 **leaf (C)**.
- Use pattern to cut 1 **leaf (D)**.

From fabric for inner pincushion:
- Cut **sides** 1¼" x 17".
- Cut **top** 4" x 4".
- Cut **bottom** 4" x 4".

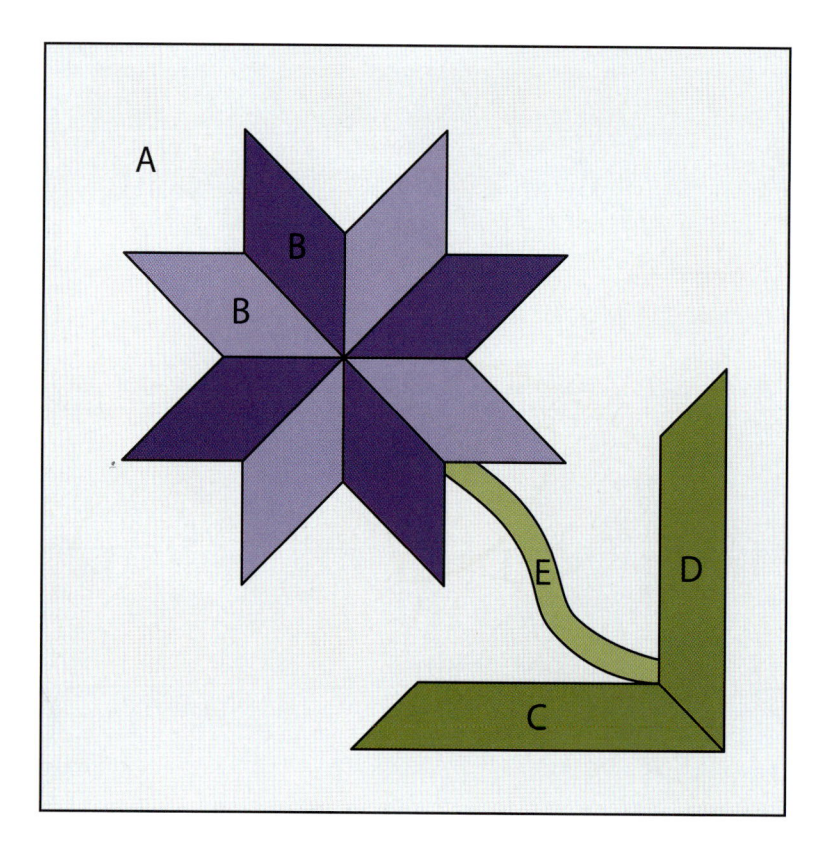

20 www.leisurearts.com

ASSEMBLY

1. Add appliqués to the **top** (**A**). We used a Running Stitch with 2 strands of dark purple floss to attach the petals and 2 strands of dark green floss to attach the leaves and stem.
2. Use 6 strands of dark purple floss to make a cluster of French Knots in the center of the petals.
3. Use Running Stitches and Straight Stitches with 1 strand of dark green floss to outline the flower.
4. Unless filling with polypropylene pellets and fiberfill, make a square dimensional inner pincushion.
5. Make and fill a square dimensional pincushion. We assembled the pincushion using a Blanket Stitch with pearl cotton.

Pole Star

Shopping List

- ☐ 1½" x 18" *or* 3" x 10" piece of light purple felt for sides
- ☐ 5" x 9" piece of dark purple felt for top and bottom
- ☐ 3" x 3" piece of green felt for triangles
- ☐ 2" x 2" piece of light pink felt for diamonds
- ☐ 2" x 2" piece of medium pink felt for diamonds
- ☐ 4" x 4" piece of dark pink felt for kite shapes
- ☐ 6" x 18" piece of fabric for inner pincushion (optional)
- ☐ embroidery floss to match green, light pink, medium pink, and dark pink felt
- ☐ #8 pearl cotton to match green felt
- ☐ general supplies

CUTTING

Measurements include ¼" seam allowances where needed. Pieces can be cut as listed or using the pattern, below.

From light purple felt:
- Cut **sides** 1¼" x 17" *or* 2 **sides** 1¼" x 9".

From dark purple felt:
- Cut **top** 4" x 4" (**A**).
- Cut **bottom** 4" x 4" (**A**).

From green felt:
- Cut 4 squares 1" x 1". Cut each square diagonally to make a total of 8 **triangles** (**B**).

From light pink felt:
- Use pattern to cut 4 **diamonds** (**D**).

From medium pink felt:
- Use pattern to cut 4 **diamonds** (**D**).

From dark pink felt:
- Use pattern to cut 8 **kite shapes** (**C**).

From fabric for inner pincushion:
- Cut **sides** 1¼" x 17".
- Cut **top** 4" x 4".
- Cut **bottom** 4" x 4".

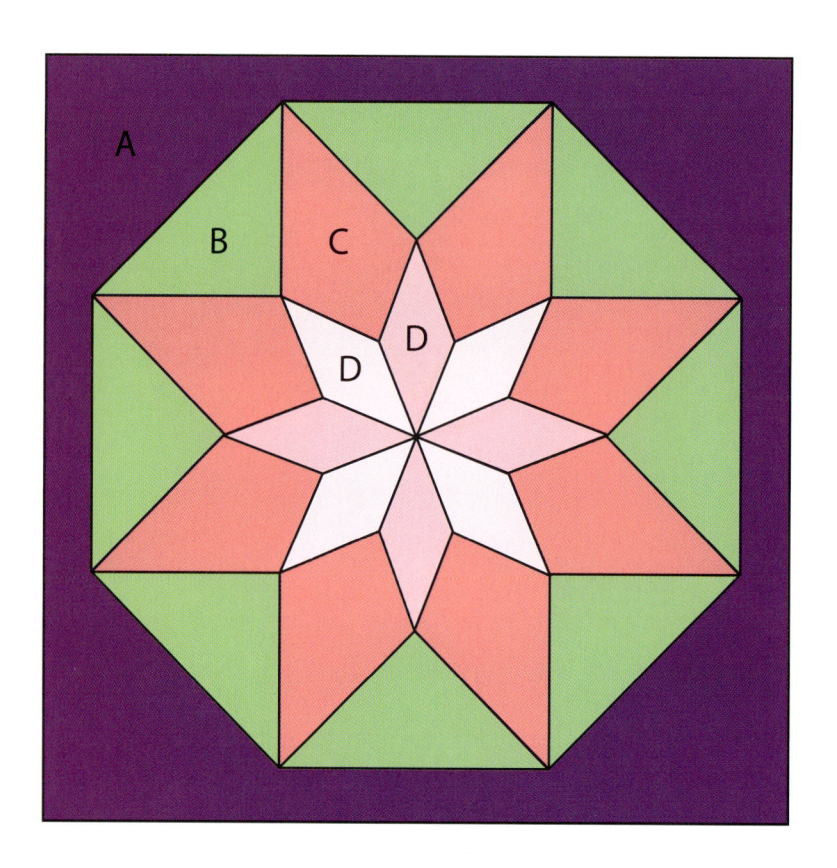

ASSEMBLY
1. Add appliqués to the **top** (**A**). We used a Running Stitch with 2 strands of embroidery floss to match the appliqués.
2. Unless filling with polypropylene pellets and fiberfill, make a square dimensional inner pincushion.
3. Make and fill a square dimensional pincushion. We assembled the pincushion using a Blanket Stitch with pearl cotton.

Western Star

Shopping List

- ☐ 2" x 2" piece of red felt for triangles
- ☐ 5" x 9" piece of dark red felt for top and bottom
- ☐ 1 1/2" x 14" *or* two 1 1/2" x 8" pieces of teal felt for sides
- ☐ 2" x 2" piece of blue felt for triangles
- ☐ 3" x 3" piece of light orange felt for diamonds
- ☐ 3" x 3" piece of orange felt for diamonds
- ☐ 6" x 14" piece of fabric for inner pincushion (optional)
- ☐ embroidery floss to match red, blue, light orange, and orange felt
- ☐ #5 pearl cotton to match orange felt
- ☐ general supplies

CUTTING

Measurements include 1/4" seam allowances where needed. Pieces can be cut as listed or using the pattern, below.

From red felt:
- Cut 4 squares 3/4" x 3/4". Cut each square diagonally to make a total of 8 **triangles (B)**.

From dark red felt:
- Use pattern to cut **top (A)** and **bottom (A)**.

From teal felt:
- Cut **sides** 1 1/4" x 13" *or* 2 **sides** 1 1/4" x 7".

From blue felt:
- Cut 4 squares 3/4" x 3/4". Cut each square diagonally to make a total of 8 **triangles (B)**.

From light orange felt:
- Use pattern to cut 4 **diamonds (C)**.

From orange felt:
- Use pattern to cut 4 **diamonds (C)**.

From fabric for inner pincushion:
- Cut **sides** 1 1/4" x 13".
- Use pattern to cut **top** and **bottom**.

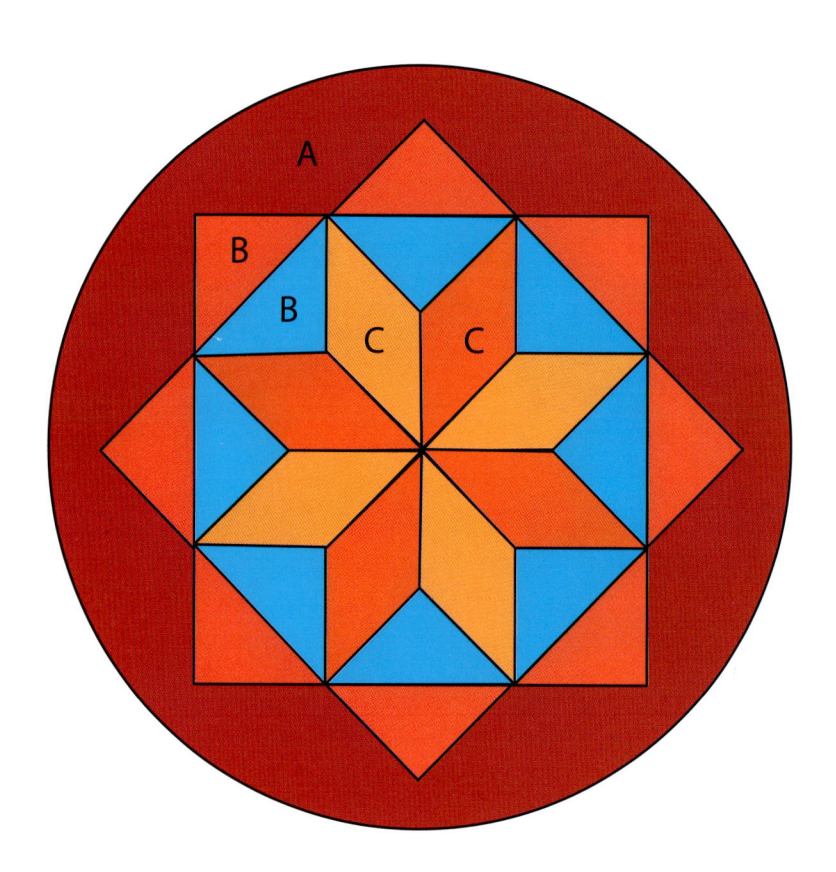

ASSEMBLY

1. Add appliqués to the **top** (**A**). We used a Running Stitch with 2 strands of embroidery floss to match the appliqués. We didn't stitch the outer edges of the red triangles.
2. Unless filling with polypropylene pellets and fiberfill, make a round dimensional inner pincushion.
3. Make and fill a round dimensional pincushion. We assembled the pincushion using a Blanket Stitch with pearl cotton.

Mariner's Compass

Shopping List

- ☐ 2½" x 4" piece of white felt for triangles
- ☐ 2½" x 4" piece of purple felt for triangles
- ☐ 5" x 5" piece of dark purple felt for bottom
- ☐ 5" x 5" piece of green felt for top
- ☐ 4" x 14" piece of fuchsia felt for triangles and sides
- ☐ 6" x 14" piece of fabric for inner pincushion (optional)
- ☐ embroidery floss to match white, purple, and fuchsia felt
- ☐ #5 pearl cotton to match fuchsia felt
- ☐ general supplies

CUTTING

Measurements include ¼" seam allowances where needed. Pieces can be cut as listed or using the pattern, below.

From white felt:
- Use pattern to cut 4 **triangles (C)**.
- Use pattern to cut 4 **triangles (E)**.

From purple felt:
- Use pattern to cut 4 **triangles (B)**.

From dark purple felt:
- Use pattern to cut **bottom (A)**.

From green felt:
- Use pattern to cut **top (A)**.

From fuchsia felt:
- Cut **sides** 1¼" x 13" *or* 2 **sides** 1¼" x 7".
- Use pattern to cut 4 **triangles (D)**.

From fabric for inner pincushion:
- Use pattern to cut **top** and **bottom**.
- Cut **sides** 1¼" x 13".

ASSEMBLY

1. Add appliqués to the **top (A)**. We used a Running Stitch with 2 strands of embroidery floss to match the appliqués.
2. Unless filling with polypropylene pellets and fiberfill, make a round dimensional inner pincushion.
3. Make and fill a round dimensional pincushion. We assembled the pincushion using a Blanket Stitch with pearl cotton.

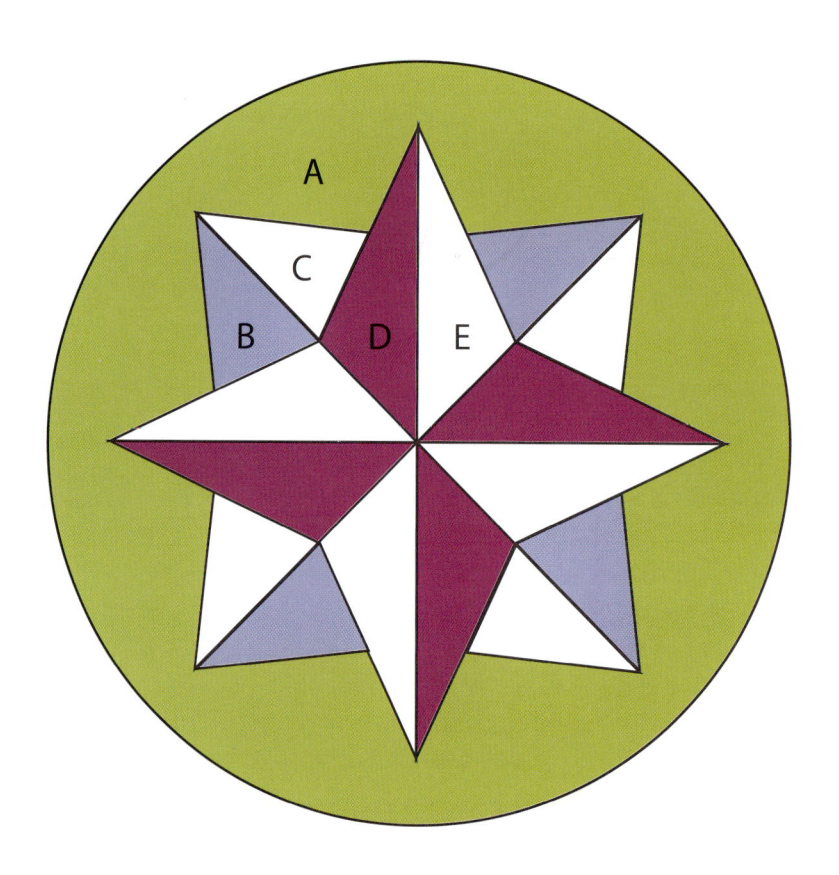

27

Bay Leaf

Shopping List

- ☐ 3" x 14" *or* 4¼" x 8" piece of green felt for sides and leaves
- ☐ 5" x 9" piece of dark green felt for top and bottom
- ☐ 2" x 2" piece of yellow felt for flower centers
- ☐ 4" x 6" piece of dark pink felt for petals
- ☐ 6" x 14" piece of fabric for inner pincushion (optional)
- ☐ embroidery floss to match green, yellow, and dark pink felt
- ☐ #5 pearl cotton to match dark pink felt
- ☐ general supplies

CUTTING

Measurements include ¼" seam allowances where needed. Pieces can be cut as listed or using the pattern, below.

From green felt:
- Use pattern to cut 4 **leaves** (**B**).
- Cut **sides** 1¼" x 13" *or* 2 **sides** 1¼" x 7".

From dark green felt:
- Use pattern to cut **top** (**A**) and **bottom** (**A**).

From yellow felt:
- Use pattern to cut 4 **flower centers** (**C**).

From dark pink felt:
- Use pattern to cut 16 **petals** (**B**).

From fabric for inner pincushion:
- Cut **sides** 1¼" x 13".
- Use pattern to cut **top** and **bottom**.

ASSEMBLY

1. Add appliqués to the **top** (**A**) and sides. We used a Running Stitch with 2 strands of embroidery floss to match the appliqués (**B**) and 3 small Straight Stitches with 2 strands of embroidery floss to stitch the appliqués (**C**).
2. Unless filling with polypropylene pellets and fiberfill, make a round dimensional inner pincushion.
3. Make and fill a round dimensional pincushion. We assembled the pincushion using a Blanket Stitch with pearl cotton.

29

Sun Goddess

Shopping List

- ☐ 5" x 9" piece of dark red felt for top and bottom
- ☐ 2" x 2" piece of yellow felt for center
- ☐ 2" x 4" piece of light orange felt for triangles
- ☐ 2" x 3$\frac{1}{2}$" piece of medium orange felt for triangles
- ☐ 1$\frac{1}{2}$" x 14" piece *or* two 1$\frac{1}{2}$" x 8" pieces of dark orange felt for sides
- ☐ 3" x 3" piece of green felt for triangles
- ☐ 6" x 14" piece of fabric for inner pincushion (optional)
- ☐ embroidery floss to match yellow, light orange, medium orange, and green felt
- ☐ #8 pearl cotton to match light orange felt
- ☐ general supplies

CUTTING

Measurements include $\frac{1}{4}$" seam allowances where needed. Pieces can be cut as listed or using the pattern, below.

From dark red felt:
- Use pattern to cut **top (A)** and **bottom (A)**.

From yellow felt:
- Use pattern to cut **center (E)**.

From light orange felt:
- Use pattern to cut 4 **large triangles (D)**.

From medium orange felt:
- Use pattern to cut 4 **medium triangles (C)**.

From dark orange felt:
- Cut **sides** 1$\frac{1}{4}$" x 13" **or** 2 **sides** 1$\frac{1}{4}$" x 7".

From green felt:
- Use pattern to cut 8 **small triangles (B)**.

From fabric for inner pincushion:
- Cut **sides** 1$\frac{1}{4}$" x 13".
- Use pattern to cut **top** and **bottom**.

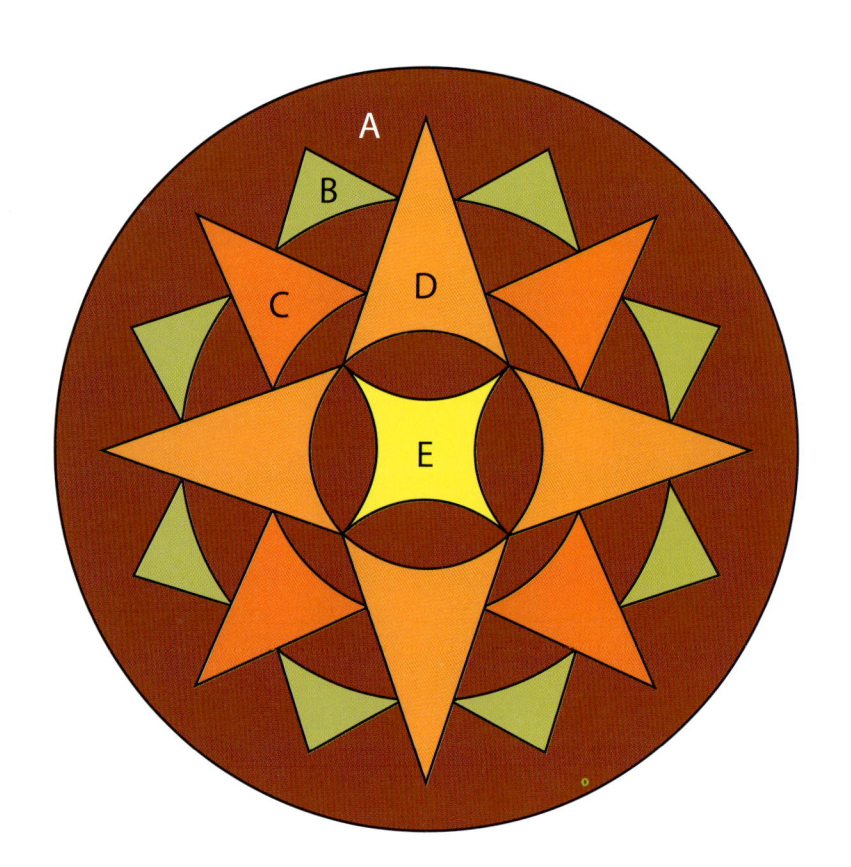

30 www.leisurearts.com

ASSEMBLY

1. Add appliqués to the **top** (**A**). We used a Running Stitch with 2 strands of embroidery floss to match the appliqués.
2. Unless filling with polypropylene pellets and fiberfill, make a round dimensional inner pincushion.
3. Make and fill a round dimensional pincushion. We assembled the pincushion using a Blanket Stitch with pearl cotton.

Meet the Designer:
Barbara B. Suess

Sewing and embroidering since childhood, Barbara B. Suess enjoys designing unique variations on objects normally found around the home, such as pincushions, potholders, trivets, pillows, and quilts.

"I've always loved handwork with fibers," she says. "It's hard for me to sit and watch TV without having some busy work for my hands." Naturally, her pincushion is never far away.

"I do a lot of embroidery, so I am using my pincushion every day. Disappointed in commercially available pincushions, I decided to make my own. I had a box of quality wool felt left over from my daughters' craft projects to use as the material. When writing my book *Japanese Kimekomi*, I had researched quilt block designs and had already diagrammed many blocks that were easy to transfer to patterns for the pincushions."

Japanese Kimekomi by Breckling Press is one of three books Barbara has written on her favorite type of embroidery, Japanese temari. She was introduced to the ancient handicraft of creating intricate thread balls in the late 1980s while living with her husband and young daughter in Yokohama, Japan. Those four years in the Far East were filled with many happy times spent sharing her love of quilting, sewing, and embroidery with Japanese friends.

Upon returning to the United States, she tried making her first temari and quickly became enthralled with the range and beauty of temari patterns. A self-taught expert, it was not long before she expanded her talents to writing temari patterns, teaching classes, and creating temari-inspired jewelry. In 2015, she achieved master/instructor certification with the Japan Temari Association based in Tokyo.

"I enjoy keeping my website (japanesetemari.com) up-to-date with my current creative projects," she says.

"My husband just retired from 35 years of working at a great job so our life is changing now," she says. "Everything is so much fun! We have two daughters who've grown into wonderful young women with busy and productive lives. We spend many hours on our dock on the Pamlico River in North Carolina enjoying the view, fishing, and passing the time with friends."

Production Team: Technical Editor – Lisa Lancaster; Technical Associate – Mary Sullivan Hutcheson; Editorial Writer - Susan Frantz Wiles; Senior Graphic Artist – Lora Puls; Graphic Artist - Cailen Cochran; Photostylist – Lori Wenger; Photographer - Jason Masters.

We have made every effort to ensure that these instructions are accurate and complete. We cannot, however, be responsible for human error, typographical mistakes, or variations in individual work.

Copyright © 2016 by Leisure Arts, Inc., 104 Champs Blvd., STE 100, Maumelle, AR 72113, www.leisurearts.com. All rights reserved. This publication is protected under federal copyright laws. Reproduction or distribution of this publication or any other Leisure Arts publication, including publications which are out of print, is prohibited unless specifically authorized. This includes, but is not limited to, any form of reproduction or distribution on or through the Internet, including posting, scanning, or e-mail transmission.